Jobs in the Arctic

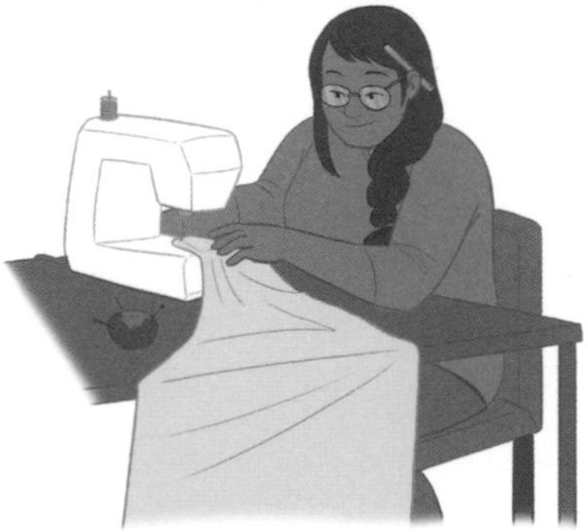

ILLUSTRATED BY

Amanda Sandland

teacher

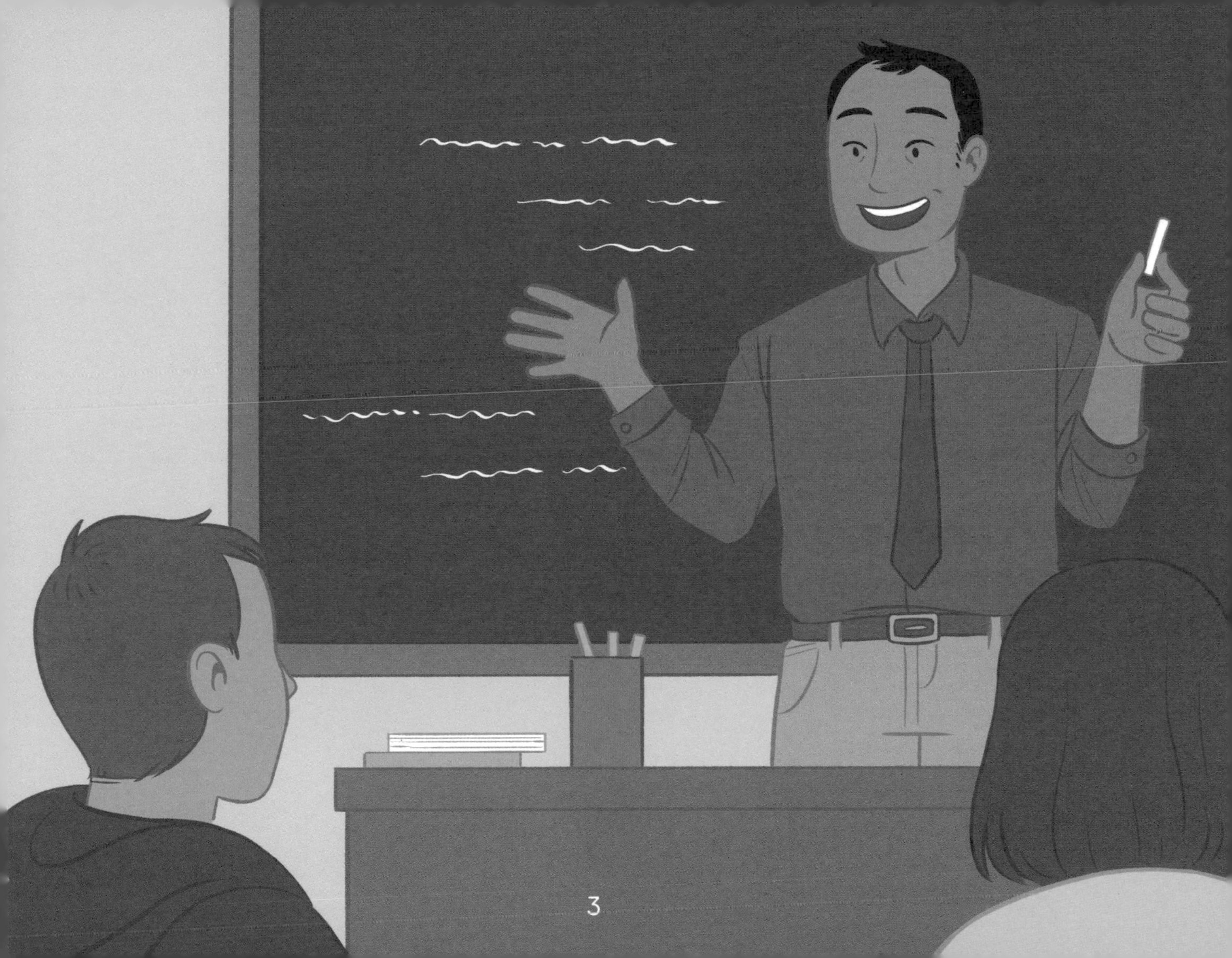

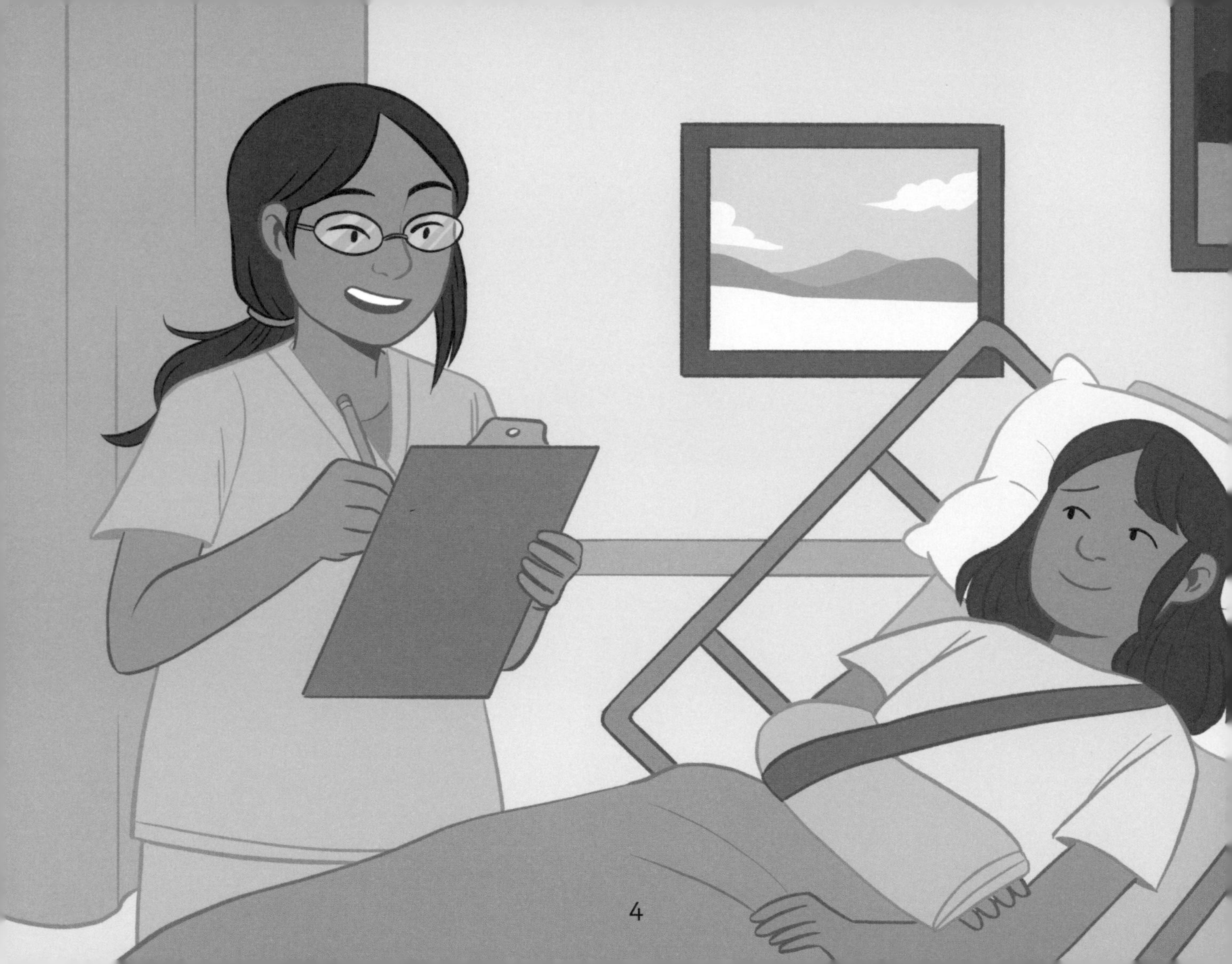

nurse

hunter

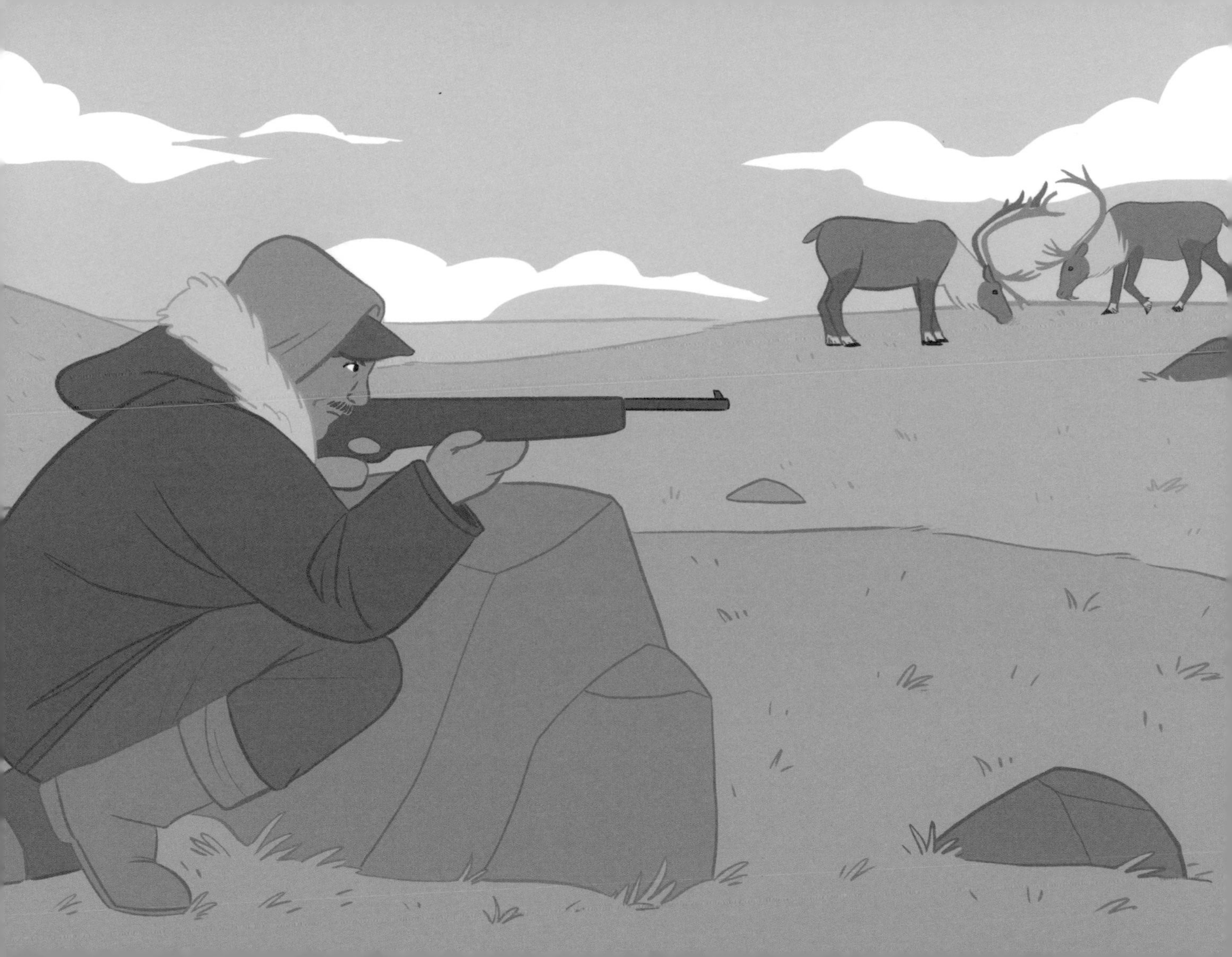

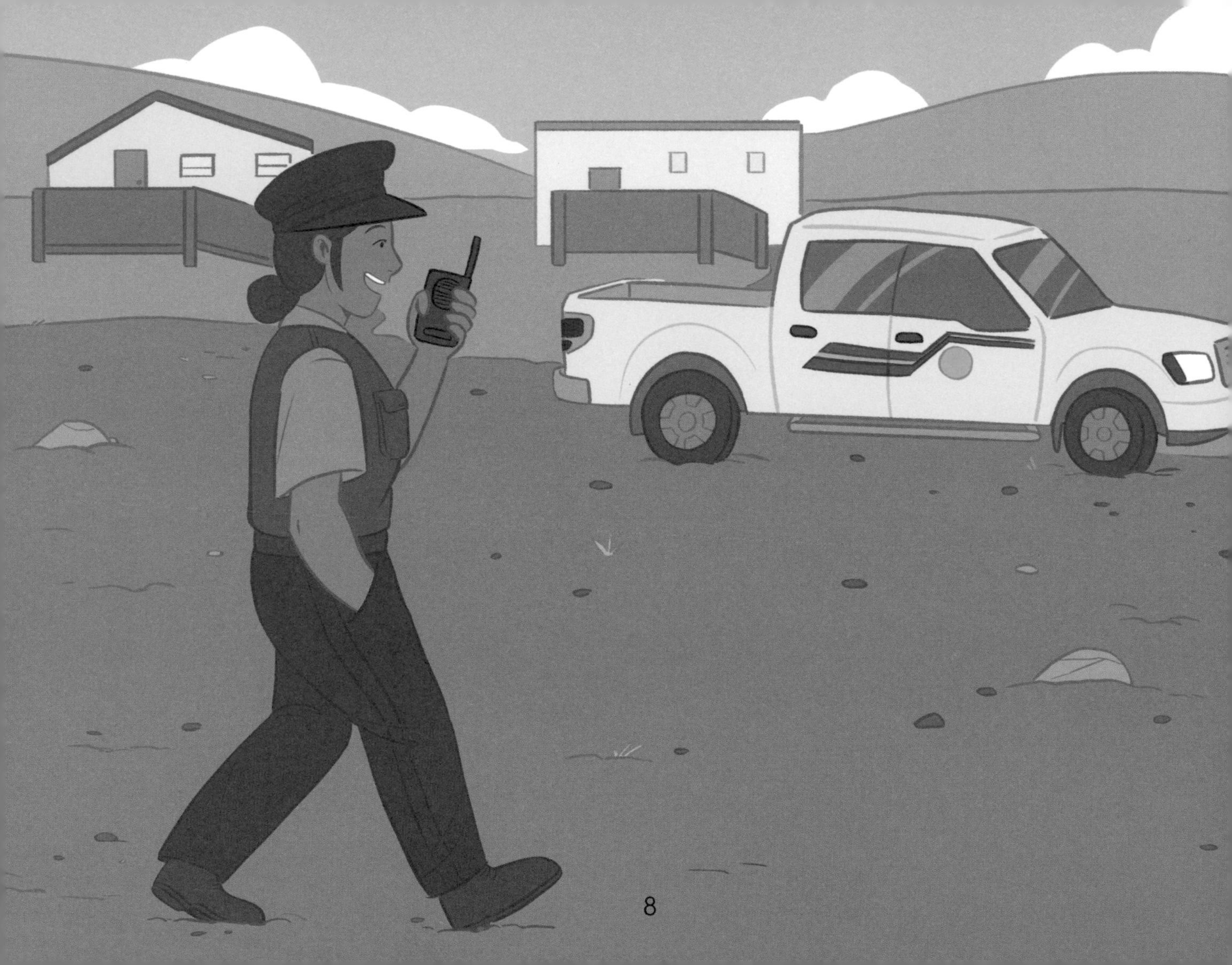

police officer

clerk

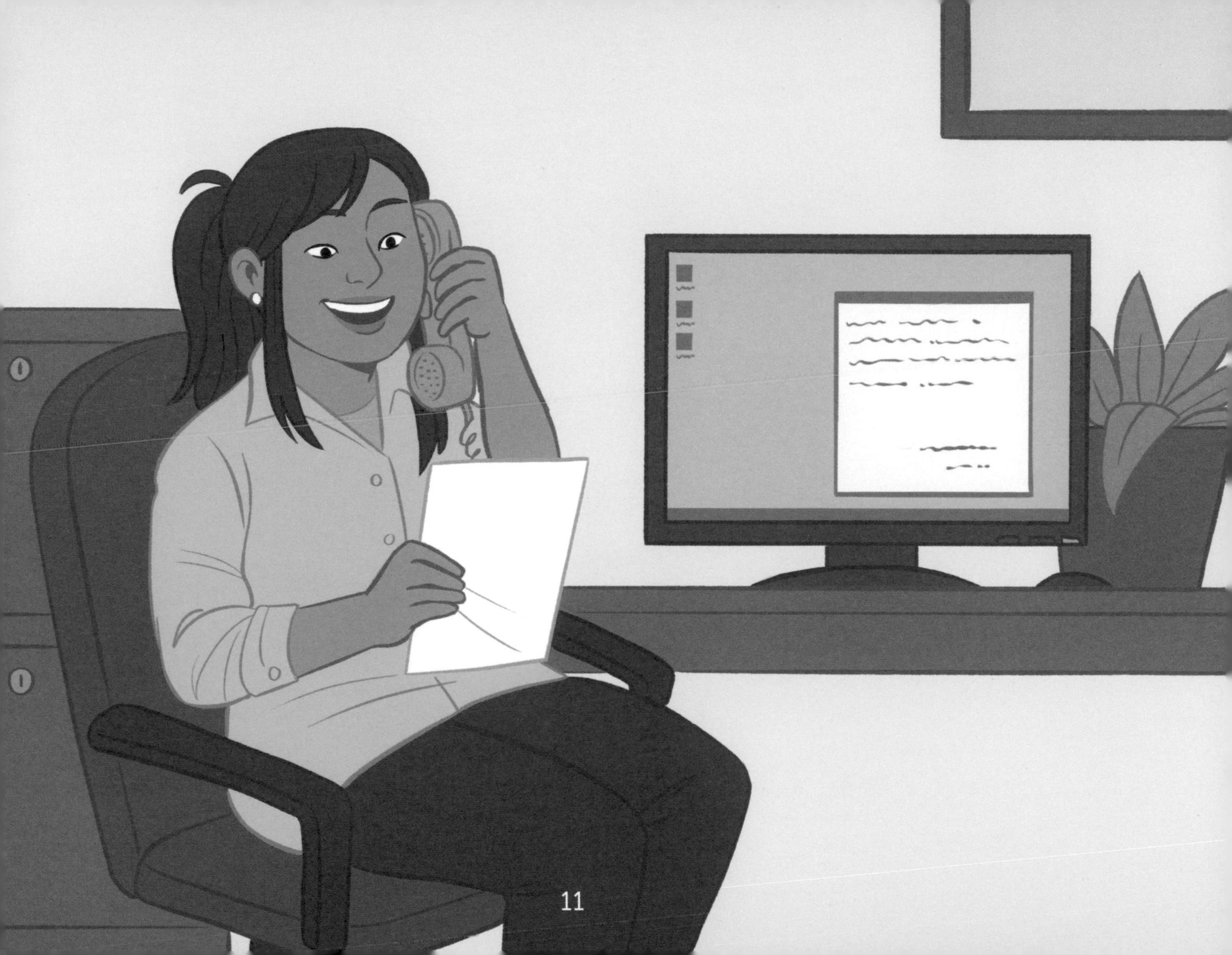

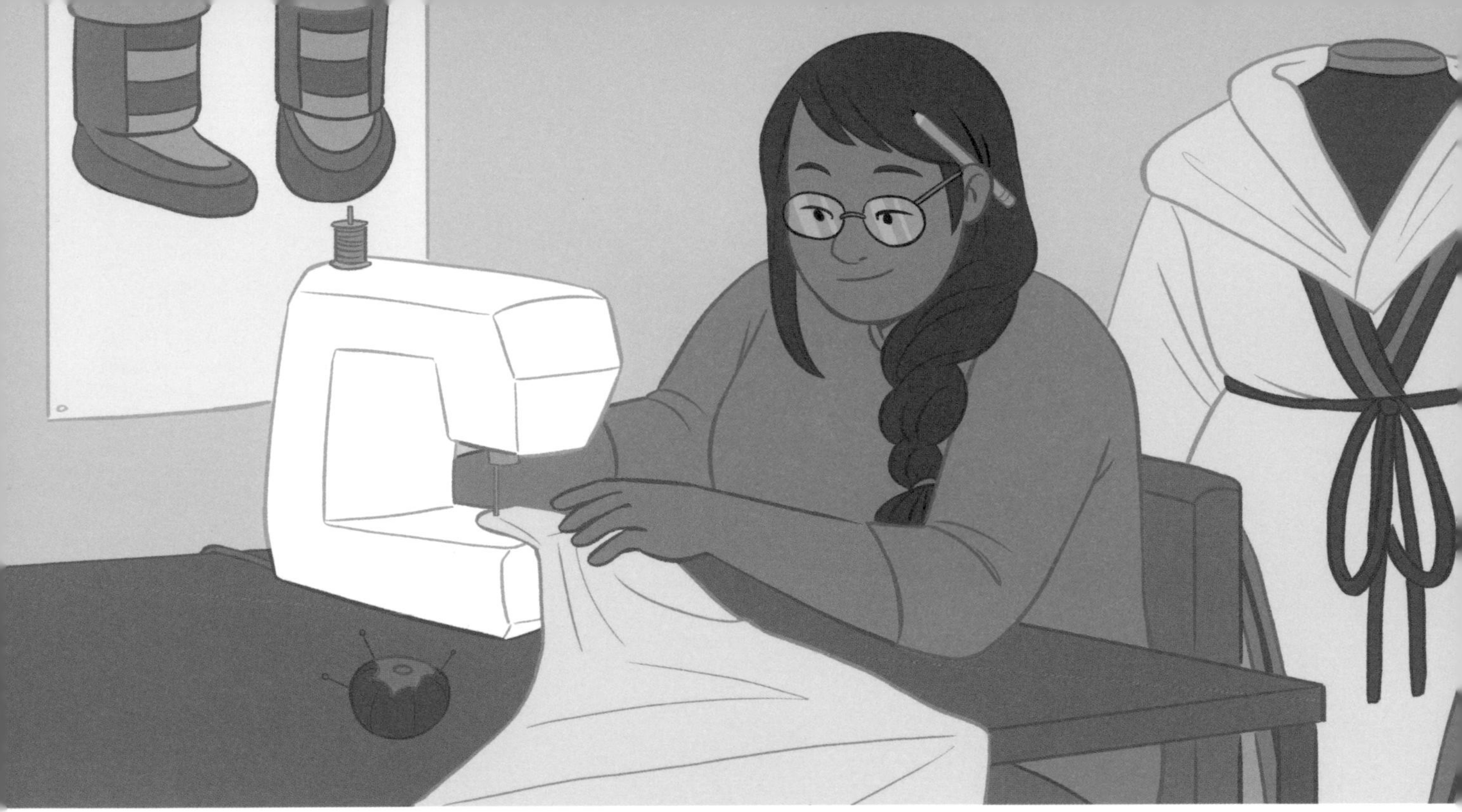

seamstress